VITAMIN
RICH

CLB 2439
© 1991 Colour Library Books Ltd, Godalming, Surrey, England
All rights reserved
This edition published in 1991 by Gallery Books,
an imprint of W.H. Smith Publishers, Inc.,
112 Madison Avenue, New York 10016
Printed and bound in Singapore
ISBN 0 8317 8049 5

Gallery Books are available for bulk purchase for sales promotions
and premium use. For details write or telephone
the Manager of Special Sales, W.H. Smith Publishers, Inc.,
112 Madison Avenue, New York, New York 10016 (212) 532-6600.

GALLERY BOOKS

Introduction

Vitamins are substances that are vital to the maintenance of our bodies, yet so much is written concerning these invisible, potent elements in our food that few of us can tell fact from fiction.

There are many different vitamins, but we only need each in very small quantities, and if we maintain a well balanced and varied diet, the food we eat will generally provide us with more than enough vitamins for our daily needs. In certain circumstances, however, such as during pregnancy, illness or in old age, vitamin supplements may be required, and in these cases professional advice should be sought.

Vitamins are mainly identified by letter, but this in no way indicates their order of importance. In the case of vitamin B, there are several complex variations of vitamins within the one heading, and this is called the "B complex". The table below gives general guidance on some of the main vitamins, their source and function.

VITAMIN	SOURCE	FUNCTION
A	Oily fish, fats, offal, carrots, green vegetables, tomatoes, watercress	General growth, good eyesight, healthy skin
B.1	Yeast extract, wheatgerm, peanuts, whole-wheat bread, eggs, pulses	Assists the nervous system and metabolism. Is water soluble and therefore easily lost in cooking
B.2	Milk, dairy products, almonds, mushrooms, pulses, red meat, green vegetables	Assists the metabolism and maintains health of mouth, lips and skin
B.3	Milk, eggs, yeast extract, red meat, dried apricots	Essential to the nervous system
B.6	Yeast, whole cereal products, offal, dairy products, bananas, leaf vegetables	Helps production of new cells and promotes nervous health
B.12	Offal, meat, eggs, cheese, milk	Assists the production of red blood cells
C	Fruit and vegetables	Helps the body resist infection, promotes good skin, helps absorption of iron
D	Oily fish, fats, dairy products, offal, red meat	Helps promote strong bones and teeth. Is produced in the body when there is exposure to sunlight
E	Whole cereal products, eggs, nuts, vegetable oil and whole-wheat flour	Necessary for upkeep of blood cells, tissues and membranes
K	Widely available in many foods such as green vegetables, eggs and cereals	Helps blood to clot and assists in the healing of wounds

SERVES 6-8

COUNTRYSIDE TERRINE

This impressive terrine looks very professional yet is simple to make.

1lb pigs' liver, ground
¾lb lean pork, ground
½lb pork sausagemeat
1 clove garlic, minced
2 shallots, finely chopped
3¾ tbsps Cognac
¾ tsp ground allspice
Salt and freshly ground black pepper
1¼ tsps chopped fresh thyme or sage
½lb bacon, rind and any bones removed
2½ tbsps heavy cream
¼lb smoked tongue or ham, cut into ¼-inch cubes
1 large bay leaf

1. Preheat oven to 350°F.

2. In a large bowl, mix together the ground liver and pork, sausagemeat, garlic, shallots, Cognac, allspice, salt, pepper, and thyme. Stir with a wooden spoon until the ingredients are evenly mixed, but still coarse in texture.

3. Lay the strips of bacon on a flat surface and stretch them with the back of a knife.

4. Line a 2lb loaf pan evenly with the strips of bacon, overlapping each strip slightly to avoid any of the terrine mixture pushing through during cooking.

5. Add the cream, cubed tongue and ham to the liver and pork mixture, blending with your hands to keep the texture coarse.

6. Press the terrine mixture into the bacon-lined loaf pan, spreading it evenly, and pushing down lightly to remove any air bubbles.

7. Place the bay leaf on the top and fold over any overlapping edges of bacon.

8. Cover the dish with a tight-fitting lid or two layers of aluminum foil.

9. Stand the loaf pan in a roasting pan and pour enough water around it to come halfway up the sides of the dish.

10. Bake the terrine for 2 hours, or until the juices run clear when a knife is inserted into the center.

11. Remove the lid or foil and replace this with some fresh foil.

12. Weigh down the terrine with cans of food or balance scale weights. Allow the terrine to cool at room temperature, then refrigerate it overnight if possible, still weighted, until it is completely chilled and firm.

13. To serve, remove the weights and foil and carefully turn the terrine out onto a serving plate. Scrape away any fat or jelly that may be on the outside of the terrine, and cut into slices just before serving.

Step 4 Line a 2lb loaf pan evenly with the strips of bacon, overlapping each strip slightly.

Step 12 Cover the terrine with a double thickness of fresh foil and weight it down with cans or scale weights.

Cook's Notes

Time
Preparation takes about 25 minutes, plus refrigeration time. Cooking takes approximately 2 hours.

Freezing
This recipe will freeze well for up to 3 months. It should be packed in plastic wrap and not aluminum or metal foil.

Vitamin Content
This recipe is an extremely good source of all the B complex vitamins.

SERVES 4

TARAMASALATA

This well known, classic Greek appetizer is a delicious way of improving your intake of vitamins B and C.

¼ cup smoked cod roe
6 slices white bread, crusts removed
1 lemon
1 small onion, finely chopped
7½ tbsps olive oil
Black olives and chopped fresh parsley, for garnish

1. Cut the cod roe in half and scrape out the center into a bowl. Discard the skin.

Step 1 Cut the cods roe in half and carefully remove the soft insides using a small spoon. Discard the skin.

2. Put the bread into a bowl along with ⅔ cup warm water. Allow the bread to soak for about 10 minutes, then drain off the water and squeeze the bread until it is almost dry. Add the bread to the bowl containing the cod roe.

3. Squeeze the lemon and add the juice to the bread and roe, stirring it well.

4. Put the cod roe mixture into a blender or food processor, along with the onion. Process until the ingredients form a smooth paste.

Step 2 Squeeze the soaked bread to remove the excess moisture.

Step 5 Gradually add the oil to the fish mixture, beating continuously and very vigorously between additions to prevent curdling.

5. Return the blended cod roe mixture to a bowl and gradually beat in the oil, a little at a time, as if making mayonnaise. Beat the mixture very thoroughly between additions with an eggbeater or wooden spoon.

6. Refrigerate the taramasalata for at least ½ hour to chill thoroughly.

7. Transfer the mixture to a serving bowl and garnish with the black olives and chopped parsley.

Cook's Notes

Time
Preparation takes about 15-25 minutes, plus refrigeration time.

Cook's Tip
Prepare the taramasalata in advance, but remove it from the refrigerator 20 minutes before serving.

Serving Idea
Warm pitta breads and toasts, cut into fingers and used for dipping, make an excellent accompaniment.

Watchpoint
Do not add the oil too quickly or the mixture will curdle. If it does, add a little more soaked bread to draw it back together again.

Vitamin Content
Vitamin B complex and also vitamin C.

SERVES 4

WATERCRESS SOUP

Watercress is packed with vitamins A, C and K, and makes delicious soup.

¼ cup butter
1 leek, cleaned and thinly sliced
½lb potatoes, peeled and sliced thinly
2½ cups chicken stock
Pinch grated nutmeg
Salt and freshly ground black pepper
4 good bunches of watercress, washed and trimmed
3¾ tbsps cream
Few extra sprigs of watercress for garnish

1. Melt the butter in a large saucepan and gently cook the leek until it is just soft, stirring frequently to prevent it from browning.

2. Add the potatoes, stock, nutmeg and seasoning to the saucepan. Bring to the boil, then cover and simmer for 15 minutes.

3. Add the watercress and simmer for a further 10 minutes.

4. Cool the soup slightly, then using a food processor or blender, process until the vegetables are very finely chopped. Rinse the saucepan and stand a fine meshed sieve over the cleaned pan.

5. Push the puréed soup through the sieve using the back of a wooden spoon, working the watercress and vegetables through the mesh until only the tough stalks remain and the soup in the pan is a fine purée.

6. Adjust the seasoning and stir the cream into the soup. Reheat gently, taking care not to boil it. Serve garnished with the reserved watercress sprigs and a little cream if desired.

Step 1 Slowly soften the leek in the melted butter, stirring to prevent it from browning.

Step 4 Blend the soup in a food processor or liquidizer until the vegetables are very finely chopped.

Step 5 Push the soup through a fine meshed sieve using a wooden spoon, work the vegetable pulp through until only the tough stalks remain in the sieve.

Cook's Notes

Time
Preparation takes 15 minutes, cooking takes about 45 minutes.

Serving Idea
Chill the soup, and serve on a bed of crushed ice for a delicious variation.

Vitamin Content
Watercress is an excellent source of vitamins A, C and K.

SERVES 4

GAZPACHO

Gazpacho is a typically Spanish soup which is served well chilled, accompanied by a selection of fresh vegetables.

1lb ripe tomatoes
1 onion, peeled and chopped
1 green pepper, seeded and diced
½ cucumber, chopped
2½ tbsps stale white breadcrumbs
2 cloves garlic, minced
2½ tbsps red wine vinegar
2½ cups tomato juice
Salt and freshly ground black pepper

Accompaniments
½ cucumber, diced
10 green onions, chopped
½lb tomatoes, skinned, seeded and chopped
1 large green pepper, seeded and diced

1. Cut a small cross in the top of each of the ripe tomatoes, and plunge into a bowl of boiling water for a few seconds.

2. Carefully peel the skin away from the blanched tomatoes. Discard the skin and roughly chop the tomatoes, removing the tough stalk as you do.

3. Put the roughly chopped tomatoes into a liquidizer or food processor, along with the onion, pepper and cucumber. Blend until finely chopped.

4. Put the chopped vegetables into a bowl with the breadcrumbs, garlic, vinegar and tomato juice. Mix well to blend evenly and allow to stand for 15 minutes.

5. Season the tomato soup thoroughly, then push through a fine meshed sieve using the back of a wooden spoon and working well to press all the vegetables through, but keeping the pips out of the resulting purée.

6. Chill the soup well before serving, surrounded by bowls containing the accompaniments.

Step 2 Carefully peel the skin away from the blanched tomatoes using a sharp knife.

Step 5 Push the puréed vegetables through a nylon sieve using the back of a wooden spoon, working until all the pulp has been pressed through and the tomato pips remain.

Cook's Notes

 Time
Preparation takes approximately 20 minutes, plus chiling time.

 Serving Idea
Serve the individual bowls of soup on crushed ice.

 Freezing
This soup is ideal for freezing.

 Vitamin Content
Extremely high in vitamin C and the tomatoes are a good source of vitamin A.

SERVES 4

MUSSEL SOUP

Shellfish contain a multitude of vitamins and minerals, especially vitamins A, E, D and K, and this soup is, therefore, a delicious way of making sure you have a good supply of all of these.

2 quarts fresh mussels
¼ cup butter
2 onions, peeled and finely chopped
2 cloves garlic, minced
1¼ cups dry white wine
1¼ cups water
2½ tbsps lemon juice
1 cup fresh white breadcrumbs
2½ tbsps freshly chopped parsley
Salt and freshly ground black pepper

1. Scrub the mussels with a stiff brush and remove any barnacle shells or pieces of seaweed that are attached to them.

2. Tap each mussel sharply to make sure that it closes tightly.

3. Melt the butter in a large saucepan and gently fry the onions and garlic until they are soft, but not browned.

4. Add the mussels, wine, water and lemon juice to the pan, and bring to the boil. Season with salt and pepper,

then cover and cook for approximately 10 minutes or until all the mussel shells have completely opened.

5. Discard any mussels which have not opened fully.

6. Strain the mussels through a colander and return the juices and stock to the saucepan. Put the mussels in a serving tureen and keep warm.

7. Add the breadcrumbs and the parsley to the mussel juices and bring them to the boil. Adjust the seasoning, and serve over the mussels in the tureen. Serve immediately.

Step 2 Tap each mussel sharply with the handle of a knife to make sure that they shut tightly. Discard any that do not.

Step 1 Scrub the mussels with a stiff brush, removing any barnacles and pieces of seaweed which may be attached to the shells.

Step 4 Cook the mussels until they have all completely opened. Discard any that remain closed.

Cook's Notes

 Time
Preparation takes 15 minutes, cooking takes approximately 20 minutes.

 Watchpoint
When cooking fresh mussels, great care must be taken to ensure that they are safe to eat. Discard any that do not shut tightly before cooking, or do not open after cooking.

 Serving Idea
Serve with warm French bread.

 Vitamin Content
This soup contains vitamins A, B, E and K.

SERVES 4-6

SPINACH GNOCCHI

Gnocchi are delicious spinach and cheese dumplings which can be served as a healthy appetizer or snack.

¼lb chopped, frozen spinach
½lb ricotta cheese, crumbled
6 tbsps Parmesan cheese, finely grated
Salt and freshly ground pepper
Pinch freshly grated nutmeg
1 egg, lightly beaten
3½ tbsps butter

1. Defrost the spinach and press it between two plates to extract all the moisture.

Step 1 Press the spinach between two plates to remove excess moisture

2. Mix the spinach with the ricotta cheese, half the Parmesan cheese, the salt, pepper and nutmeg. Gradually add the egg, beating well until the mixture holds together when shaped.

3. With floured hands, shape the mixture into oval shapes. Use about 1 tbsp mixture for each gnocchi.

4. Lower into simmering water 3 or 4 at a time and allow to cook gently until the gnocchi float to the surface (about 1-2 minutes).

5. Remove with a draining spoon and place in a well buttered ovenproof dish.

6. When all the gnocchi are cooked, sprinkle on the re-

Step 3 Shape the gnocchi mixture with well-floured hands into ovals or balls.

Step 4 The gnocchi will float to the surface of the water when cooked. Remove with a draining spoon.

maining Parmesan cheese and dot with the remaining butter.

7. Reheat for 10 minutes in a hot oven and brown under a preheated broiler before serving.

Cook's Notes

Time
Preparation takes 15 minutes, cooking takes about 20 minutes.

Variation
Accompany with a tomato or cheese sauce and a salad for a light meal.

Vitamin Content
Spinach is a good source of vitamin A and the cheese provides vitamin B.

SERVES 4

ZUCCHINI SALAD

Raw vegetables are full of vitamins, and zucchini in particular has a delicious taste and texture.

½lb macaroni
4 tomatoes
4-5 zucchini, sliced thinly
8 stuffed green olives, sliced
7½ tbsps French dressing

1. Put the macaroni into a large saucepan and cover with boiling water. Add a little salt and simmer for 10 minutes, or until tender but still firm. Rinse in cold water and drain well.

2. Cut a small cross in the tops of each tomato and plunge into boiling water for 30 seconds.

3. Carefully remove the skins from the blanched tomatoes, using a sharp knife. Chop the tomatoes coarsely.

4. Mix all the ingredients in a large bowl and chill in the refrigerator for 30 minutes before serving.

Step 1 Rinse the macaroni in lots of cold water, then drain well forking it occasionally to prevent it sticking together.

Step 4 Mix all the ingredients together well, stirring thoroughly to blend the dressing in evenly.

Cook's Notes

Time
Preparation takes 15 minutes, cooking takes approximately 10 minutes.

Variation
Use any other pasta shape of your choice.

Preparation
If you prefer, the zucchini can be blanched in boiling water for 1 minute, then drained and cooled before mixing with the salad ingredients.

Vitamin Content
This recipe is high in vitamin C from the zucchini and tomatoes, vitamin A from the tomatoes and vitamin B from the pasta.

SERVES 4-6

WATERCRESS AND ORANGE SALAD

This colorful salad combination is ideal served with cold meats or fish.

3 large bunches of watercress
4 oranges
7½ tbsps vegetable oil
Juice and rind of 1 orange
Pinch sugar
1¼ tsps lemon juice
Salt and freshly ground black pepper

1. Wash the watercress and carefully cut away any thick stalks. Break the watercress into small sprigs, discarding any yellow leaves.

2. Carefully remove the peel and pith from the oranges using a sharp knife. Catch any juice that spills in a small bowl.

3. Cutting carefully, remove the fleshy segments from between the thin membrane inside the orange. Squeeze any juice from the orange membrane into the bowl with the juice from the peel.

4. Arrange the watercress with the orange segments on a serving dish.

5. Put the remaining ingredients into the bowl with the reserved orange juice, and mix together well.

6. Pour the salad dressing over the oranges and watercress just before serving, to prevent the watercress from going limp.

Step 2 Carefully peel the oranges using a sharp knife, and collecting any juices in a small bowl.

Step 1 Break the watercress into small sprigs, discarding any yellow leaves.

Step 3 Cut the orange segments carefully from between the inner membranes using a sharp knife.

Cook's Notes

Time
Preparation takes approximately 20 minutes.

Serving Idea
Serve this salad on a bed of finely grated carrot.

Variation
Use grapefruit instead of the oranges, and chicory instead of the watercress.

Vitamin Content
This salad is extremely high in vitamin C, and if served with carrot is also a good source of vitamin A.

SERVES 4

CHEESE SALAD

This cheese salad is distinctly Greek in origin, and is ideal as an appetizer as well as being substantial enough to serve as a light lunch.

½ small head of endive or Crisp lettuce
½ small Iceberg lettuce
1 small cucumber
4 large tomatoes
8-10 pitted green or black olives, halved
1 medium-sized Spanish or red onion, peeled and sliced
¼lb feta cheese
6 tbsps olive oil
2½ tbsps red wine vinegar
1¼ tsps chopped fresh oregano
¾ tsp freshly ground sea salt
½ tsp freshly ground black pepper
¾ tsp ready made German mustard

1. Wash the endive and lettuce leaves thoroughly. Pat them dry with paper towels and tear into bite-sized pieces.

2. Thinly slice the cucumber, peeling it if you wish.

3. Cut a small cross into the top of each tomato and plunge into boiling water for 30 seconds.

4. Carefully peel the skins from the blanched tomatoes and slice the flesh crosswise.

5. Put the endive, lettuce, cucumber, tomatoes, olives and onion into a serving bowl and toss them together until well mixed.

6. Cut the feta cheese into ½-inch cubes. Sprinkle these

Step 1 Tear the lettuce and endive into pieces to prevent excessive bruising and destruction of vitamins in the leaves.

Step 4 Using a sharp knife, slice the peeled tomatoes crosswise.

cubes over the salad in the serving bowl.

7. Put all the remaining ingredients into a small bowl and whisk together using a fork or small eggbeater.

8. Pour the dressing over the salad and serve immediately.

Cook's Notes

Time
Preparation takes 10-12 minutes.

Serving Idea
Serve with jacket potatoes or crusty French bread.

Variation
Use Cheddar or Cheshire cheese in place of the feta cheese.

V **Vitamin Content**
Leaf vegetables such as lettuce are an excellent source of vitamin K. The tomatoes and cucumber are high in vitamin C and the cheese is a good source of vitamins B and D.

SERVES 6

ROGNONS À LA DIJONNAISE

This delicious French dish makes good use of vitamin-rich kidneys, an offal which is often underused in cookery.

½lbs lambs' kidneys
¼ cup unsalted butter
1-2 shallots, finely chopped
1¼ cups dry white wine
6 tbsps lightly salted butter, softened
3½ tbsps Dijon mustard
Salt, black pepper and lemon juice, to taste
2½ tbsps chopped parsley

Step 2 Trim away any hard core from the center of each kidney half using a small pair of sharp scissors.

Step 1 Trim the fat from each kidney and cut them in half lengthwise.

Step 8 Whisk the butter, mustard, salt, pepper and lemon juice into the reduced sauce using a fork or eggbeater and beating until it is thick.

1. Trim away any fat from the kidneys and slice them in half lengthwise.

2. Carefully snip out any hard core from the center using a pair of sharp scissors.

3. Melt the unsalted butter in a large frying pan and gently sauté the kidneys, uncovered, until they are light brown on all sides.

4. Remove the kidneys from the frying pan and keep them warm.

5. Add the shallots to the meat juices in the pan and cook

for about 1 minute, stirring frequently until they are just soft.

6. Add the wine and bring to the boil, stirring constantly and scraping the pan to remove any browned juices.

7. Boil this sauce rapidly for 3-4 minutes to reduce by about half. Remove the pan from the heat.

8. Put the softened butter into the pan with the mustard and seasonings. Whisk the mixture into the reduced sauce with an eggbeater or fork.

9. Return the pan to the heat and add the kidneys and the parsley. Heat very gently for 1-2 minutes, taking care not to boil the mixture any further. Serve immediately.

Cook's Notes

Time
Preparation takes approximately 25 minutes, cooking takes 15-17 minutes.

Watchpoint
Do not overcook the kidneys or they will become tough.

Vitamin Content
Kidneys are an excellent source of vitamins A, B and D.

SERVES 6

PORK PROVENÇALE

This hearty casserole of lean pork topped with potatoes is suitable for serving as a family meal, or as part of a dinner party menu.

2lbs pork fillets
¼ cup butter
¾lb onions, peeled and thinly sliced
15oz can tomatoes
Salt and freshly ground black pepper
½ tsp dried mixed herbs
1½lbs potatoes, peeled and thinly sliced
1 tbsp chopped parsley for garnish

1. Trim the pork of any surplus fat and slice into thin strips.

2. Melt half of the butter in a large sauté pan and gently fry

Step 1 Slice the pork into thin strips using a sharp knife.

Step 4 Gently fry the onions in the meat juices until they are just soft.

the slices of meat, stirring continuously to prevent them from burning.

3. Transfer the meat to a plate and set aside.

4. Stir the onions into the meat juices in the sauté pan and cook gently until just soft.

5. Add the tomatoes to the pan along with the salt, pepper and mixed herbs. Bring to the boil, then simmer gently for about 5 minutes, or until the sauce has reduced by about a third.

6. Arrange the meat, sauce and potatoes in layers in an ovenproof serving dish, finishing with a layer of potato.

7. Melt the remaining butter and brush the top layer of potato with this.

8. Cover the dish with a lid or foil, and cook in the oven for 1½ hours at 350°F.

9. Remove the lid from the dish and continue cooking for a further 30 minutes to brown the potatoes. Sprinkle with chopped parsley before serving.

Step 6 Arrange the meat, tomato sauce and potatoes in layers in an ovenproof serving dish.

Cook's Notes

Time
Preparation takes 25 minutes, cooking takes approximately 2 hours.

Freezing
This dish will freeze very well for up to 3 months. Freeze it before the final 30 minutes cooking time, then reheat by thawing and cooking uncovered for 1 hour at 350°F.

V **Vitamin Content**
The vegetables are a good source of vitamin C, and the tomatoes also contain vitamin A.

SERVES 4

LENTIL KEDGEREE

This delicious recipe combines spiced rice with lentils and onion to make a substantial vegetarian lunch or supper dish.

1¼ cups basmati rice
1¼ cups red lentils
3¼ cups warm water
½ cup butter, or olive oil
1 medium-sized onion, peeled and chopped
¾ tsp crushed fresh root ginger
¾ tsp minced garlic
1-inch piece cinnamon stick
6 cloves
1 bay leaf
1¼ tsps ground coriander
½ tsp ground turmeric
¾ tsp freshly ground sea salt
2 green chilies, sliced in half lengthwise

1. Wash the rice and the lentils thoroughly in cold water. Drain well.

2. Put the drained rice and lentils into a large bowl and cover with the warm water. Soak for 30 minutes, then drain very thoroughly, reserving the water.

3. Heat the butter or olive oil in a large saucepan. Stir in the onion and fry gently for 2-3 minutes, stirring to prevent it burning.

4. Add the ginger, garlic, cinnamon stick, cloves and bay leaf to the onion and continue frying for 1 minute.

5. Add the rice and lentils to the fried onion, along with the coriander, turmeric, salt and green chili. Stir over the heat for 2-3 minutes, until the rice and lentils are evenly coated

Step 5 Stir-fry the rice and lentils together, making sure that they are evenly coated with the fat.

Step 6 Cook the rice and lentils until all the liquid has been absorbed, then fluff up with a fork before serving.

with fat.

6. Pour the reserved water into the rice mixture and bring to the boil. Reduce the heat and cover the pan with a tight fitting lid. Simmer for 8-10 minutes without stirring, or until the water has been completely absorbed.

7. Stir the rice and lentils together, remove and discard the chilies, and serve immediately.

Cook's Notes

Time
Preparation takes 15 minutes, plus soaking time. Cooking takes approximately 30 minutes.

Watchpoint
Great care must be taken when using fresh chilies. If any of the juice gets into your mouth or eyes, rinse with lots of cold water.

V Vitamin Content
Lentils and rice are both excellent sources of vitamin B.

SERVES 4

LENTIL AND VEGETABLE CURRY

Lentils are a staple ingredient in Indian cookery. This delicious vegetable curry should be made using fresh spices for the best flavor.

1¼ cups whole green lentils
2½ tbsps vegetable oil
1¼ tsps salt
¾ tsp mustard seed, crushed
1 tsp ground coriander
¾ tsp ground cumin
2 dried red chilies, crushed
1 carrot, peeled and sliced diagonally
1 potato, peeled and cubed
6-8 okra, topped and tailed, then cut into 1-inch pieces
1 small zucchini, sliced diagonally
1 small eggplant, halved and sliced
1¾ cups water
6 curry leaves
1 green chili, slit in half and chopped
1¼ tsps fresh chopped mint
1¼ tbsps fresh chopped coriander
Coriander leaves for garnish

1. Wash the lentils in warm water until it runs clear. Drain well.

2. Put the lentils into a large saucepan and pour over 2½ cups water. Simmer gently for 15-20 minutes.

3. When the lentils are soft, beat with a potato masher or eggbeater until they are puréed.

4. In a large saucepan heat the oil and gently fry the mustard seed, ground coriander, cumin and dried chilies for 1 minute.

5. Add the vegetables to the spices and cook for 2 minutes, stirring all the time, to coat them evenly in the oil and spice mixture.

6. Add the water and the puréed lentils to the vegetable mixture and stir well.

7. Add the curry leaves, chopped chili, mint and fresh coriander, then cook for 15 minutes. Serve hot, garnished with coriander leaves.

Step 3 Using a potato masher or eggbeater, break up the cooked lentils until they are well puréed.

Step 6 Stir the puréed lentils into the vegetable mixture.

Cook's Notes

Time
Preparation takes about 10 minutes, cooking takes 20-30 minutes.

Variation
Use any combination of fresh vegetables to vary this curry.

Serving Idea
Serve with boiled basmati rice.

Vitamin Content
Lentils provide an excellent source of vitamin B and fresh vegetables provide vitamins A and C.

SERVES 4

BEEF WITH PINEAPPLE AND PEPPERS

This delicious sweet and sour main course is distinctly Chinese in origin.

1lb fillet or rump steak
1 small pineapple
1 green pepper
1 red pepper
1¼ tbsps peanut oil
1 onion, peeled and roughly chopped
2 cloves garlic, minced
1-inch fresh root ginger, peeled and thinly sliced
1¼ tsps sesame oil
2½ tbsps light soy sauce
1¼ tbsps dark soy sauce
1¼ tsps sugar
1¼ tbsps brown sauce
5 tbsps water
Salt and freshly ground black pepper

1. Using a sharp knife, cut the steak into thin strips.

2. Carefully peel the pineapple and cut out any eyes using a sharp knife or potato peeler. Cut the pineapple into slices and chop them into bite-sized pieces, removing the hard core.

3. Slice the green and red peppers in half. Remove and discard the cores and seeds. Chop the pepper flesh into thin strips.

4. Heat the peanut oil in a wok or large frying pan, and gently fry the onion, garlic and ginger, stirring continuously until the onion has softened slightly.

5. Add the strips of beef and the strips of pepper, and continue stir-frying for 3 minutes.

6. Add the pineapple and stir-fry again for 2 minutes.

7. Remove the meat, vegetables and fruit from the wok, and put on a plate. Set aside.

8. Stir the sesame oil into the juices in the wok and add the soy sauces, sugar, brown sauce and water. Simmer rapidly for 30 seconds to reduce and thicken.

9. Stir the fruit, vegetables and beef back into the sauce. Season, heat through and serve immediately.

Step 1 Using a sharp knife, cut the steak into thin strips.

Step 5 Stir-fry the beef and peppers with the onions in the wok.

Cook's Notes

Time
Preparation takes 30 minutes, cooking takes about 10 minutes.

Serving Idea
Serve with spring rolls and plain boiled rice.

Watchpoint
Take care not to overcook the meat and vegetables, as this will greatly reduce the vitamin content of this dish.

Vitamin Content
Steak is an excellent source of vitamin B and the vegetables and fruit are high in vitamin C.

SERVES 4

KIDNEYS WITH BACON

Stir-frying is an excellent way of cooking kidneys, as the speedy cooking ensures that they do not become tough.

1lb lambs' kidneys
2½ tbsps vegetable oil
8 strips lean bacon, cut into 1-inch strips
1 onion, peeled and chopped
3 cloves garlic, minced
1¼ tbsps tomato chutney
1¼ tbsps light soy sauce
2½ tbsps water
Salt and freshly ground black pepper
1¼ tbsps cornstarch
3¾ tbsps sherry
2 tbsps fresh chopped parsley

1. Trim the fat from the kidneys and cut each kidney in half with a sharp knife.

2. Carefully trim out the hard core from the center of each kidney with a sharp knife or scissors.

3. Cut a lattice design on the back of each kidney using a sharp knife and taking care not to cut right through.

4. Put the kidneys into a bowl and stir in the sherry. Set aside for 15 minutes to marinate.

5. Heat the oil in a large wok and fry the bacon, onion and garlic for 5 minutes, stirring continuously to prevent burning. Remove from the wok and set aside on a plate.

6. Drain the kidneys and reserve the sherry marinade. Add the kidneys to the wok and stir for 3 minutes only.

7. Stir the tomato chutney, soy sauce and water into the wok with the kidneys, then add the bacon and onion mixture. Season with salt and pepper and stir-fry gently for 5 minutes.

8. Blend the cornstarch with the sherry marinade.

9. Add 1 tbsp parsley to the cornstarch mixture and stir

Step 2 Remove the hard core from each kidney half using a sharp knife or a small pair of scissors.

Step 3 Cut a lattice design on the backs of each kidney, using a sharp knife, and taking care not to cut right through.

Step 6 Stir-fry the kidneys until they are completely browned.

this into the kidneys in the wok, mixing well until the sauce is thickened and smooth. Serve at once, sprinkled with a little extra parsley.

Cook's Notes

Time
Preparation takes 20 minutes, cooking takes 25 minutes.

Serving Idea
Serve with rice or creamed potatoes.

Vitamin Content
All offal is an excellent source of vitamins A, B and D.

SERVES 4

MONKFISH AND PEPPER KEBABS

Monkfish is ideal for making kebabs as it can be cut into firm cubes, which do not disintegrate during cooking.

8 strips of lean bacon, rind removed
1lb monkfish, skinned and cut into 1-inch pieces
1 small green pepper, seeded and cut into 1-inch pieces
1 small red pepper, seeded and cut into 1-inch pieces
12 small mushroom caps
8 bay leaves
3¾ tbsps vegetable oil
½ cup dry white wine
5 tbsps tarragon vinegar
2 shallots, finely chopped
1¼ tbsps chopped fresh tarragon
1¼ tbsps chopped fresh chervil or parsley
1 cup butter, softened
Salt and freshly ground black pepper

Step 2 Wrap each piece of fish in one of the strips of bacon.

Step 8 Add the butter gradually into the simmering wine, whisking briskly to thicken the sauce.

1. Cut the bacon strips in half lengthwise and then again in half crosswise.

2. Put a piece of the fish onto each piece of bacon and roll the bacon around the piece of fish.

3. Thread the bacon and fish rolls onto large skewers, alternating them with slices of pepper, mushroom and the bay leaves.

4. Brush the kebabs with oil and arrange on a broiler pan.

5. Preheat the broiler to hot and cook the kebabs for 10-15 minutes, turning them frequently to prevent the kebabs from burning.

6. Heat the white wine, vinegar and shallots in a small saucepan until boiling. Cook rapidly to reduce by half.

7. Add the herbs and lower the heat.

8. Using a fork or eggbeater beat the butter bit by bit into the hot wine mixture, whisking rapidly until the sauce becomes thick. Season to taste.

9. Arrange the kebabs on a serving plate and serve with a little of the sauce spooned over and the remainder in a separate jug.

Cook's Notes

Time
Preparation takes 30 minutes, cooking will take about 25 minutes.

Preparation
When making the sauce it is important to whisk briskly, or it will not thicken sufficiently.

V **Vitamin Content**
Fish is an excellent source of vitamins A and D. Bacon is a good source of vitamin B, and peppers are high in vitamin C.

SERVES 4

SWORDFISH STEAKS WITH GREEN PEPPERCORNS AND GARLIC SAUCE

Swordfish steaks are delicious and are easily available at most good fishmongers.

2½ tbsps fresh green peppercorns
7½ tbsps lemon juice
5 tbsps olive oil
Freshly ground sea salt
4 swordfish steaks
1 egg
1 clove garlic, roughly chopped
⅔ cup oil
2½ tsps fresh oregano
Salt and freshly ground black pepper

1. Crush the green peppercorns lightly using a pestle and mortar.

2. Mix the lemon juice, olive oil and salt into the lightly crushed green peppercorns.

3. Place the swordfish steaks in a shallow ovenproof dish and pour the lemon and oil mixture over each steak. Re-frigerate overnight, turning occasionally until the fish becomes opaque.

4. Using a blender or food processor, mix together the eggs and garlic.

5. With the machine still running, gradually pour the oil through the funnel in a thin steady stream onto the egg and garlic mixture. Continue to blend until the sauce is thick.

6. Remove the leaves from the oregano sprigs and chop them finely.

7. Preheat the broiler to hot and arrange the swordfish on the broiler pan.

8. Sprinkle the chopped oregano over the swordfish steaks and season well. Cook for 15 minutes, turning them frequently and basting with the lemon and pepper marinade.

9. When the steaks are cooked, place on a serving dish and spoon the garlic mayonnaise over.

Step 1 Lightly crush the green peppercorns using a pestle and mortar.

Step 3 Marinate the swordfish steaks overnight, after such time they should be opaque.

Cook's Notes

Time
Preparation takes 25 minutes, plus overnight soaking.
Cooking takes about 15 minutes.

Variation
Substitute 2½ tbsps well rinsed canned green peppercorns in place of the fresh peppercorns if you cannot get these, and use tuna steaks instead of the swordfish if you prefer.

Serving Idea
Serve with jacket potatoes and fresh salad.

Vitamin Content
The fish contains vitamins B and D.

SERVES 4

TARRAGON GRILLED RED SNAPPER

Red snapper is a very decorative little fish that is now readily available at fishmongers and supermarkets.

4 large or 8 small red snapper, cleaned, scaled, washed and dried
4 or 8 sprigs of fresh tarragon
5 tbsps vegetable oil
·2½ tbsps tarragon vinegar
Salt and freshly ground black pepper
1 egg
1¼ tsps Dijon mustard
½ cup sunflower oil
1¼ tbsps wine vinegar
1¼ tsps brandy
1¼ tbsps chopped fresh tarragon
1¼ tbsps chopped fresh parsley
1¼ tbsps heavy cream

1. Rub the inside of each fish with a teaspoonful of salt, scrubbing hard to remove any discolored membranes inside. Rinse thoroughly.

2. Place a sprig of fresh tarragon inside each fish.

3. Using a sharp knife, cut 2 diagonal slits on the side of each fish.

4. Mix together the vegetable oil, tarragon vinegar and a little salt and pepper in a small bowl.

5. Arrange the fish on a shallow dish and pour over the tarragon/vinegar marinade, brushing some of the mixture into the cuts on the side of the fish. Refrigerate for 30 minutes.

6. Put the egg into a blender or food processor along with the mustard and a little salt and pepper. Process for 2-3 seconds to mix.

7 With the machine running, add the oil through the funnel in a thin steady stream. Continue blending the dressing until it is thick and creamy.

8. Add the vinegar, brandy and herbs, and process for a further 30 seconds to mix well.

9. Lightly beat the cream with a small eggbeater until it thickens.

10. Fold the slightly thickened cream carefully into the oil and vinegar dressing. Pour into a serving dish and refrigerate until ready to use.

11. Arrange the fish on a broiler pan and cook under a preheated hot broiler for 5-8 minutes per side, depending on the size of the fish. Baste frequently with the marinade while cooking, then serve with a little of the sauce and some sprigs of fresh tarragon, if you like.

Step 1 Rub the insides of each fish with a teaspoonful of salt, scrubbing briskly to remove any discolored membranes.

Step 3 Using a sharp knife, cut 2 diagonal slits on the side of each fish, taking great care not to cut right through the flesh.

Cook's Notes

Time
Preparation takes about 15 minutes, cooking takes 10-16 minutes.

Variation
Use herrings or mackerel in place of the mullet.

Vitamin Content
All fish is an excellent source of vitamins A and D.

SERVES 4

DUCK WITH ORANGES

This traditional combination is given extra flavor by cooking the duck in a distinctly oriental manner.

3 oranges
1 duck
1 tbsp butter
1¼ tbsps oil
1¼ cups light chicken stock
⅓ cup red wine
2½ tbsps redcurrant jelly
Salt and freshly ground black pepper
1¼ tsps arrowroot
1¼ tbsps cold water

1. Using a potato peeler carefully pare the rind thinly off 2 of the oranges.

Step 2 Using a sharp knife carefully cut the parred orange rind into very thin strips.

2. Cut the rind into very fine shreds using a sharp knife. Put the shredded orange rind into a small bowl and cover with boiling water. Set aside to blanch for 5 minutes, then drain.

3. Squeeze the juice from the 2 oranges. Set this aside.

4. Cut away the peel and the pith from the remaining orange and then slice the flesh into thin rounds. Set aside.

5. Wash the duck and dry well with paper towels.

6. Put the butter and the oil into a large wok and heat until melted. Add the duck and fry, turning frequently until it is brown all over.

7. Remove the duck from the wok, cool slightly and using poultry shears, cut away the leg and wing ends. Cut the duck in half lengthwise and then cut each half into 1-inch strips.

8. Remove the fat from the wok and return the duck to the wok. Add the stock, red wine, redcurrant jelly, squeezed orange juice, and the well drained strips of rind. Bring to the boil, then season to taste. Reduce the heat, cover the

Step 7 Cut each half of the duck into 1-inch strips using poultry shears or a very sharp knife.

wok and simmer the duck gently for 20 minutes, or until well cooked.

9. Skim away any surface fat and thicken the sauce by mixing the arrowroot with the water and stirring into the wok. Bring the mixture back to the boil and simmer for a further 5 minutes, or until the sauce is thick.

10. Arrange the duck on a serving plate and garnish with the orange slices and some additional watercress if liked.

Cook's Notes

Time
Preparation takes 30 minutes, cooking takes 35 minutes.

Serving Idea
Serve with plain boiled rice or sautéed potatoes.

Vitamin Content
Duck is a good source of vitamin B, and oranges are an excellent source of vitamin C.

SERVES 4-6

LIVER WITH ONIONS

This dish is simple to prepare, but absolutely delicious and highly nutritious.

1lb onions
1lb lambs' liver, thinly sliced
Salt and freshly ground black pepper
⅓ cup all-purpose flour
3¾ tbsps vegetable oil
2 tbsps butter
2½ tbsps fresh chopped parsley

1. Peel the onions and slice thinly, keeping each slice in

Step 1 Using a sharp knife, thinly slice the peeled onions, keeping them in rings if possible.

circles if possible.

2. Trim away any large pipes or tubes from the liver using a pair of small scissors or a sharp knife.

3. Mix the seasoning and the flour together on a plate and lay the slices of liver into the flour, turning them and pressing them gently to coat all over evenly.

4. Put the oil and the butter into a large frying pan. Heat

Step 2 Trim away any pipes or tubes from the liver slices using a small pair of scissors or a sharp knife

Step 3 Coat each liver slice thoroughly with the seasoned flour, pressing it gently onto the surface.

gently until foaming.

5. Add the onion rings and fry until just golden.

6. Add the liver slices and fry for 3-5 minutes on each side until well cooked. Cooking time will depend on the thickness of each slice.

7. Stir the parsley into the liver and onions and serve immediately on hot plates.

Cook's Notes

Time
Preparation takes 15 minutes, cooking takes about 10 minutes.

Variation
Add 4 oz shredded bacon to this recipe with the onions.

Serving Idea
Serve with creamed potatoes and green vegetables.

Watchpoint
Do not overcook liver or any offal, as it will toughen.

Freezing
Liver freezes well, but should be frozen before cooking.

Vitamin Content
Onions are a good source of vitamin C. Liver is an excellent source of vitamins A, B and D.

SERVES 4

'BURNT' CREAM

The gentle cooking of this creamy dessert ensures that the valuable vitamin content in the cream is not decreased in any way.

1¼ cups whole milk
1¼ cups heavy cream
5 egg yolks
⅓ cup superfine sugar
Few drops of vanilla extract
½ cup Barbados sugar
⅔ cup whipped heavy cream (optional)

---

1. Put the milk and the cream into a heavy-based saucepan and heat gently until almost boiling. Remove from the heat and set aside to cool slightly.

2. Put the egg yolks, sugar and vanilla into a bowl and whip vigorously until they become light and creamy.

3. Strain the milk and cream through a sieve into a large jug.

4. Gradually add the strained milk and cream onto the egg yolk mixture, beating vigorously and constantly as you pour.

5. Rinse the saucepan clean and dry it. Return the egg yolk and cream mixture to the saucepan and heat gently, stirring constantly with a wooden spoon, until the mixture becomes a thick and creamy custard.

6. Do not allow the custard to boil or it will curdle.

7. Strain the custard through a sieve into a shallow serving dish. The custard should come almost to the top of the dish.

8. Stand the custard in a refrigerator and chill until set, preferably overnight.

9. Sprinkle the brown sugar thickly over the surface of the set custard

10. Stand the custard under a preheated hot broiler and cook until the sugar melts and caramelizes. Remove the 'burnt cream' from the broiler and chill it until the sugar layer is a hard, crisp caramel.

11. Serve very cold, decorated with piped heavy cream if desired.

Step 2 Whip the egg yolk, sugar and vanilla together until thick and creamy. The mixture is ready when you can leave a trail on the surface as it is lifted with a spoon or eggbeater.

Step 10 Broil the brown sugar on the top of the chilled custard until it melts and caramelizes.

Cook's Notes

Time
Preparation takes about 15 minutes, cooking takes about 30 minutes, plus chiling time.

Preparation
The custard is ready when the mixture coats the back of a wooden spoon.

Watchpoint
Take great care never to boil the mixture at any stage, or it will curdle. If this should happen, blend 2 tbsps cornstarch with a little milk and stir this into the hot curdled mixture, continue stirring until it thickens and becomes smooth.

Serving Idea
Serve with crisp crackers or a fresh fruit salad.

Vitamin Content
Cream and milk contain vitamins A, B and D. Never expose cream or milk to sunlight, as this will destroy the valuable vitamin B.

SERVES 4

RICE PUDDING

Rice pudding has always been a firm family favorite and this recipe adds spices to make it special enough even for dinner parties.

¼ cup unsalted butter
1 bay leaf, crumbled
1-inch piece cinnamon stick, crushed
1 cup pudding rice, washed and drained
5 cups milk
1¾ cups evaporated milk
¾ cup granulated sugar
½ cup chopped blanched almonds
Seeds of 8 small cardamoms, crushed
¼ cup pistachio nuts, chopped or cut into slivers

1. Melt the butter in a saucepan and fry the bay leaf and cinnamon for 1 minute.

2. Add the rice and stir well to coat evenly with the melted fat.

3. Add the milk and bring the mixture to the boil, then reduce the heat and simmer for 40-50 minutes, stirring occasionally to prevent the rice from sticking to the pan.

4. Add the sugar and the evaporated milk to the rice mixture and continue cooking for a further 20-30 minutes, stirring frequently to prevent burning.

5. It is important to keep stirring the mixture during this cooking time to bring up thin layers of light brown skin which form on the base of the saucepan. This is what gives the pudding its rich, reddish tinge and caramel flavor.

6. Add the chopped almonds and the crushed cardamom seeds to the rice puddings. Stir well and pour into a large serving dish.

7. Decorate the top of the rice pudding with the slivered pistachio nuts, and serve hot or cold.

Step 5 Stir the pudding frequently to bring up the thin layers of light brown skin which will form on the base of the saucepan during cooking.

Step 2 Stir the rice into the fried bay leaf and cinnamon, mixing well to coat each grain evenly with the flavored fat.

Step 7 Decorate the pudding with slivered pistachios before serving.

Cook's Notes

Time
Preparation takes 10 minutes, cooking takes 1 hour 30 minutes.

Watchpoint
Frequent stirring is important in this recipe to prevent the sugar from caramelizing too much and giving a bitter flavor to the dessert.

Vitamin Content
Rice contains vitamins from the B group, and milk and evaporated milk contain vitamins A and D.

SERVES 4-6

SUMMER PUDDING

This favorite summer dessert simply oozes vitamins and flavor.

1½lbs fresh soft fruit, e.g. raspberries, strawberries, rhubarb, redcurrants, blackcurrants or any combination of these fruits
¾ cup granulated sugar
10 thick slices of white bread, crusts removed
1¾ cups fresh cream
1lb fresh whole raspberries

1. Put the 1½lbs of mixed fruit into a large saucepan and stir in the sugar.

2. Heat the fruit gently, shaking the pan vigorously so that the sugar dissolves but the fruit stays as intact as possible. Remove from the heat and cool completely.

3. Cut the slices of bread into thick fingers and use them to line the base and sides of a medium-sized mixing bowl. Press the slices of bread together as firmly as possible to avoid leaving any gaps between them.

4. Pour the cooled fruit and the juice into the center of the pudding, and cover the top completely with the remaining bread. Press down firmly.

5. Place a saucer or small plate over the top of the pudding and weigh this down with cans of food or balance scale weights.

6. Chill the pudding overnight in the refrigerator.

7. Remove the weights and the small plate or saucer. Loosen the sides of the pudding carefully with a round bladed knife, and invert a serving plate over the top of the bowl.

8. Carefully turn both the serving plate and the bowl over, and shake gently. The pudding should drop onto the serving plate.

9. Whip the cream until it is thick, then spread approximately half of the cream over the summer pudding.

Step 2 Shake the fruit and sugar together gently over a low heat until the sugar dissolves, but the fruit remains mainly intact.

Step 3 Press the slices of bread together well around the sides and the base of the mixing bowl, trying to make sure that there are no gaps in between each slice.

Step 10 Press the whole raspberries into the cream layer covering the summer pudding.

10. Press the fresh raspberries onto the cream in a thick layer all over the pudding, and pipe the remaining cream in small rosettes between the gaps.

11. Chill well, before serving.

Cook's Notes

Time
Preparation takes approximately 30 minutes, plus overnight chiling.

Freezing
This pudding freezes extremely well, but should be decorated with the fruit and cream after it has been thawed.

V Vitamin Content
The bread contains vitamin B, the fruit contains vitamin C, and the cream contains vitamin D.

SERVES 4-6

CARROTELLA

Carrots have a natural sweetness which lends itself to sweet as well as savory dishes. Carrotella is a sweet and spicy dessert which should be served very cold.

5 cups milk
1lb carrots, peeled and finely grated
1 cup evaporated milk
½ cup granulated sugar
⅓ cup golden raisins
Seeds of 8 small cardamoms, crushed
2 drops vanilla extract
¼ cup chopped blanched almonds
¼ cup chopped pistachio nuts

1. Put the milk into a saucepan and simmer over a low heat until reduced to about 3½ cups.

2. Add the carrots. Cover and cook over a medium heat for approximately 15 minutes, or until the carrots have begun to soften.

3. Stir in the evaporated milk, sugar and golden raisins, re-cover and simmer gently for about another 5 minutes.

4. Remove the saucepan from the heat, then stir in the crushed cardamom seed and vanilla essence.

5. Beat the carrotella briskly to break up the carrots, then turn into a serving dish and cool slightly.

6. Sprinkle the nuts on top and chill very well before serving.

Step 2 Cook the carrots over a medium heat for 15 minutes, or until they have softened and are breaking up.

Step 6 Sprinkle the partially chilled carrotella with the chopped nuts.

Cook's Notes

Time
Preparation takes 15 minutes. Cooking takes 40 minutes, plus chiling time.

Serving Idea
Serve with a spoonful of chilled fromage frais.

Variation
Use rosewater instead of the vanilla extract, and finely chopped hazelnuts instead of the pistachio nuts.

V **Vitamin Content**
Milk and evaporated milk contain vitamins D and E. Carrots are an excellent source of vitamins A and C.

SERVES 4

BROWN BREAD ICE CREAM

This unusual ice cream is easy to make and is an ideal standby dessert to keep in the freezer.

2 egg yolks
⅓ cup superfine sugar
2 cups heavy or whipping cream
Few drops of vanilla extract
½ cup water
½ cup Barbados sugar
7 tbsps fresh brown breadcrumbs
1¼ tsps ground cinnamon

1. Put the egg yolks and the superfine sugar into a bowl, and whisk vigorously with an electric beater until thick, pale and creamy.

2. Pour in the heavy cream and continue whisking until thick and creamy.

3. Beat in the vanilla extract, then pour the cream mixture into a freezer-proof container and freeze for 1 hour, or until beginning to set around the edges.

4. Break the ice cream away from the edges and whisk with the electric beater until the ice crystals have broken. Return to the freezer and chill for a further hour. Repeat this procedure 2 more times, then freeze completely.

5. Put the water and the brown sugar into a small saucepan and heat gently, stirring until the sugar has dissolved. Bring the mixture to the boil and boil rapidly until the sugar caramelizes.

6. Remove the caramel sugar from the heat and stir in the breadcrumbs and the cinnamon.

7. Spread the caramel mixture onto a cookie sheet lined with oiled wax paper, and allow to set.

8. Break up the caramelized breadcrumbs by placing

Step 1 Whisk the eggs and superfine sugar together until they are pale, thick and creamy.

Step 7 When cooled, the caramelized breadcrumbs should set completely hard.

them in plastic food bags and crushing with a rolling pin.

9. Turn the frozen ice cream into a large bowl and break it up with a fork.

10. Allow the ice cream to soften slightly, then stir in the caramelized breadcrumbs, mixing thoroughly to blend evenly.

11. Return the brown bread ice cream to the freezer tray and freeze completely.

12. Allow the mixture to soften for 10 minutes before serving in scoops.

Cook's Notes

Time
Preparation takes approximately 40 minutes, plus freezing time.

Preparation
Be very careful when making the caramel sugar as it can burn very easily.

V **Vitamin Content**
Wholemeal bread contains vitamins B and E. Fresh cream contains vitamins A, B and D.

SERVES 4-6

FRUITY BREAD PUDDING

This traditional family pudding is made extra nutritious by using whole-wheat bread and a rich assortment of dried fruits.

¾ cup raisins
¾ cup currants
¾ cup golden raisins
¾ cup prunes, stoned and chopped
Finely grated rind and juice of 1 orange
8 thick slices whole-wheat bread, crusts removed
¼ cup butter, softened
½ cup Barbados sugar
1¼ cups whole milk
2 eggs, lightly beaten
½ tsp ground nutmeg
½ tsp ground cinnamon

1. Put all the dried fruit, orange rind and orange juice into a large bowl and mix well.

2. Put about half of the mixed fruit into the base of a lightly buttered ovenproof serving dish.

3. Spread the bread with the butter and cut it into small squares.

4. Arrange half of the bread squares over the fruit in the

Step 3 Cut the buttered bread into squares approximately 2 inches.

base of the serving dish.

5. Sprinkle with half of the brown sugar, then repeat the layers once again, finishing with a layer of sugar.

6. Whisk together the milk, eggs, nutmeg and cinnamon. Pour the mixture over the bread pudding and allow to stand for 1 hour.

7. Bake the pudding in a preheated oven, 375°F, for about 35-40 minutes, or until crisp on top but still soft at the bottom. Serve very hot.

Step 5 Arrange the fruit, bread and sugar in layers in an ovenproof dish.

Step 6 Pour the egg and milk mixture over the bread and fruit, taking care not to dislodge the pieces of bread.

Cook's Notes

Time
Preparation takes 15 minutes, plus 1 hour soaking. Cooking takes 40 minutes.

Freezing
This pudding will freeze well and should be reheated for 20 minutes in a hot oven, 375°F. Cover the top with foil to prevent it from burning or browning further.

Vitamin Content
Dried fruit is an excellent source of vitamin C, and milk and eggs are good sources of vitamins A, B, D and E. Whole-wheat bread is an excellent source of vitamins B and E.

SERVES 4

CARAMEL ORANGES

Rich in vitamins A and C, oranges need very little preparation to provide a delicious dessert.

4 large oranges
1½ cups granulated sugar
1¼ cups water
4 tbsps boiling water
2½ tbsps Cointreau

1. Using a potato peeler or very sharp knife, carefully pare the peel only from the oranges. Cut this peel into very thin strips, removing any white pith as you do so.

2. Put the orange peel strips into a small bowl and cover with boiling water. Allow to stand for 20 minutes, then drain.

3. Carefully peel all the pith from the oranges with a serrated edged knife. Cut the oranges horizontally into slices approximately ¼-inch thick. Reserve any juice which spills in a small jug.

4. Put the orange juice, the 1¼ cups water and sugar into a small saucepan, and heat gently all the time until the sugar has dissolved.

5. Increase the temperature and bring the sugar syrup to the boil, boiling rapidly until it turns a pale gold color.

6. Remove the caramel from the heat and quickly stir in the 4 tbsps of boiling water.

7. Add the orange rind to the sugar syrup along with the Cointreau, and allow to cool completely.

8. Arrange the orange slices in a serving dish, and pour over the cooled syrup. Chill for several hours or overnight, before serving.

Step 1 Cut the parred orange rind into very thin julienne strips with a sharp knife.

Step 3 Carefully remove all the white pith from the oranges, using a serrated knife and cutting with a sawing action.

Step 5 Cook the sugar and the syrup over a moderate heat, until it turns pale gold in color. Take care not to overcook at this stage.

Cook's Notes

Time
Preparation takes 25 minutes, cooking takes 20 minutes.

Watchpoint
Take care not to overcook the sugar syrup or it will burn and spoil the flavor.

Preparation
Hold the pan slightly away from you when adding the boiling water, as the syrup will splutter and spit and can give a very nasty burn.

Freezing
Fresh oranges freeze very well, but sugar syrup should be made fresh each time.

Vitamin Content
Oranges are an excellent source of vitamins A and C.

MAKES 1 x 10-INCH LOAF

CARROT CAKE

Carrots give a cake a delicious sweet flavor, as well as lots of vitamins and minerals. What better excuse do you need to indulge in this delicious tea-time treat.

¾ cup butter
¾ cup Barbados sugar
2 eggs, well beaten
2 cups all-purpose whole-wheat flour
2 tsps baking soda
¾ tsp baking powder
½ tsp ground cinnamon
½ tsp ground nutmeg
¾ tsp salt
½lb peeled carrots, grated
⅔ cup raisins
½ cup finely chopped walnuts
½ tsp cardamom seeds, crushed
Confectioners' sugar, for dredging

1. Beat the butter and sugar together until they are light and fluffy.

2. Add the eggs a little at a time, beating well and adding a teaspoonful of the flour with each addition, to prevent the mixture from curdling.

3. Put the remaining flour into a large bowl along with the bicarbonate of soda, baking powder, cinnamon, nutmeg and salt. Mix together well.

4. Carefully fold the flour into the butter and egg mixture, mixing well to ensure that it is blended evenly.

5. Add the carrots, raisins, nuts and cardamom seeds, beating the mixture well to blend evenly.

6. Lightly grease a 10-inch loaf pan and line the base with a piece of silicone paper.

7. Pour the cake mixture into the loaf pan, and bake in a preheated oven 350°F, for 45-50 minutes or until a fine metal skewer comes out clean when inserted into the center of the cake.

8. Cool the cake in its pan for 15 minutes before turning out onto a wire rack to cool completely.

9. Dredge the cake with confectioners' sugar just before serving.

Step 2 Beat the eggs gradually into the butter and sugar, adding a little flour with each addition to prevent the mixture from curdling.

Step 5 Stir the carrots, fruit and nuts into the cake mixture, mixing well to blend evenly.

Cook's Notes

Time
Preparation takes 30 minutes, cooking takes 45-50 minutes.

Watchpoint
If the egg and butter mixture should curdle, add a little more flour and beat very hard with an electric whisk until the curdling disappears.

V Vitamin Content
Whole-wheat flour is an excellent source of vitamins B and D. Carrots are an excellent source of vitamins A and C.

MAKES 1 x 8-INCH CAKE

TOASTED ALMOND CAKE

A crunchy toasted almond topping makes this cake very different from run-of-the-mill tea-time treats.

⅔ cup butter, softened
½ cup superfine sugar
2 eggs, lightly beaten
1½ cups whole-wheat self-rising flour
¾ tsp vanilla extract
2½ tbsps orange juice
⅓ cup Barbados sugar
¼ cup melted, unsalted butter
1¼ tbsps milk
½ cup slivered almonds
½ cup confectioners' sugar
2½ tbsps cornstarch
3 egg yolks
½ cup milk
⅓ cup heavy cream, whipped
½ tsp almond extract

1. Beat the butter and superfine sugar until it is light and fluffy.

2. Beat in the eggs one at a time, adding a teaspoonful of the flour with each addition to prevent the mixture from curdling.

3. Fold in all the remaining flour, along with the vanilla extract and the orange juice.

4. Lightly grease a 8-inch cake pan, and line the base with a piece of silicone paper.

5. Spoon the cake mixture into the pan and spread the top evenly with a palette knife.

6. Put the brown sugar into a small saucepan, along with the melted butter, the 1¼ tbsps milk and the slivered almonds. Stir over a low heat until the sugar has completely dissolved.

7. Sprinkle about 1¼ tbsps of additional flour over the top of the cake mixture in the pan, then pour over the melted sugar, butter and almond mixture. Spread it evenly, but try not to disturb the cake mixture too much.

8. Bake the cake in a preheated oven 375°F for 20-30 minutes, or until the cake is well risen and the topping has caramelized golden brown.

9. Put the confectioners' sugar, cornstarch and egg yolks into a bowl, and using an electric beater, whisk until they are light and fluffy.

10. Pour on the milk, gradually whisking between additions. Strain this egg yolk mixture through a sieve into a heavy-based saucepan.

11. Cook the egg yolk and milk mixture over a gentle heat until it begins to thicken, and will thickly coat the back of a wooden spoon. Stir the mixture frequently during the cooking time to prevent it from burning or curdling.

12. Remove from the heat and cool.

13. When the custard is completely cool, lightly fold in the cream and the almond extract.

14. When the cake has cooled, carefully cut it in half horizontally with a sharp knife. Sandwich the two halves back together using the almond custard as a filling.

15. Chill thoroughly before serving.

Cook's Notes

Time
Preparation takes 40 minutes. Cooking takes about 30 minutes, plus 10 minutes for the filling.

Watchpoint
Do not allow the almond topping to become too hot. Heat it just long enough to dissolve the sugar. If it does overheat, allow it to cool before pouring onto the uncooked cake mixture.

Vitamin Content
Whole-wheat flour contains B group vitamins and vitamin E. Nuts contain vitamins B and E, and butter and eggs contain vitamins A, B, D and E. Milk and cream contain vitamins A and D.

MAKES 1 x 8-INCH CAKE

CINNAMON BUTTER CREAM CAKE

This sumptuous cake has the added advantage of requiring no cooking.

1⅓ cup granulated sugar
¾ tsp ground cinnamon
7½ tbsps water
8 egg yolks
2 cups unsalted butter, softened
48 ladyfingers
10 tbsps brandy
1 cup toasted almonds, roughly chopped
1 cup unsweetened chocolate, coarsely grated

Step 9 Line the cake pan with trimmed ladyfingers and spread with approximately half of the buttercream.

1. Put the sugar, water and cinnamon in a small heavy-based saucepan and bring to the boil, stirring constantly until the sugar dissolves.

2. Allow the sugar syrup to boil briskly without stirring, until it begins to thicken, but has not browned. This temperature should be 236°F on a sugar thermometer; or when the sugar mixture will form a small ball when dropped into a bowl of cold water.

3. Beat the egg yolks in a large bowl with an electric mixer, until they are pale and thick.

4. Pour the sugar syrup quickly, in a thin steady stream, into the whisked egg yolks, beating constantly with the electric beater.

5. Continue beating in this way until the mixture is thick, smooth and creamy. Allow to cool at room temperature.

6. Still using the electric mixer, beat the softened butter a spoonful at a time, into the egg and sugar mixture. Beat well to ensure that it is evenly distributed. Chill the mixture until it reaches spreading consistency.

7. Line an 8-inch square pan with greased foil or silicone paper.

8. Cut the ladyfingers into neat pieces to enable you to use them to line the cake pan.

9. Divide the butter cream in half and spread a little of the buttercream lightly on one side of each biscuit and place them, icing side down, into the pan.

10. Cut any small pieces of biscuits to fill any corners, if necessary.

11. Continue spreading the buttercream on the ladyfingers and lining the cake pan in this way, alternating the direction of the fingers between the layers.

12. Sprinkle half of the brandy over the ladyfingers, then continue spreading the remainder of the sponge with just half of the buttercream and filling the cake pan completely. Sprinkle with the remaining brandy, then chill in the refrigerator overnight.

13. Remove the cake from the pan and peel off the paper or foil. Slide the cake onto a flat surface and coat with the remaining half of the buttercream.

14. Press the chopped almonds on to the sides of the cake and decorate the top with the grated chocolate. Serve immediately, or chill in the refrigerator until required.

Cook's Notes

Time
Preparation takes about 45 minutes, plus overnight chiling.

Freezing
This cake freezes well.

Variation
The icing may be flavored with 2 tsps instant coffee powder, which should be added when making the syrup.

Vitamin Content
Butter contains vitamins A, B and D, and eggs contain vitamins B and E. Nuts contain vitamins B and E.

Index

COMPILED BY PATRICIA PAYNE
EDITED BY JILLIAN STEWART
PHOTOGRAPHY BY PETER BARRY
RECIPES STYLED BY HELEN BURDETT
DESIGNED BY TINA LEE
COVER DESIGN BY MARILYN O'NEONS